GROSS ME OUT!

GROSS SMELLS

Darla Duhaime

Guided Reading Level: P

Rourke
Educational Media

rourkeeducationalmedia.com

Scan for Related Titles and
Teacher Resources

TABLE OF CONTENTS

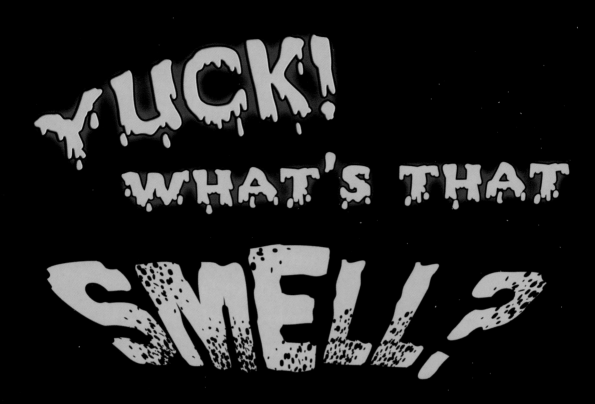

YUCK! WHAT'S THAT SMELL?

On your way into a restaurant, you walk by its dumpster. The **putrid** scent of rotting garbage fills your nose. Pee-yew! There goes your appetite!

About four percent of human genes are dedicated to smell.

4

What's the grossest thing you've ever smelled? Do you know why it smells that way? Here's a hint: science has the answer!

THAT'S ROTTEN

When spoiled food begins to stink, **microbes** such as yeasts, bacteria, and mold are often to blame.

The **pungent** odors either come from chemicals released by the food as the microbes decompose it, or from chemicals the microbes produce.

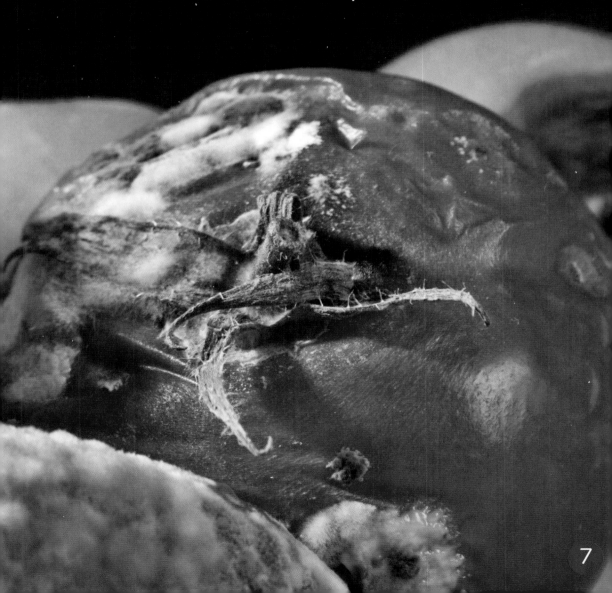

Some scientists think microbes produce stinky chemicals to deter other animals from eating the food. That way, they don't have to share!

Microorganisms use the water in foods to fuel the chemical reactions they need to break down the food for their own energy and growth. If they make it stink in the process, their food source likely won't be eaten by anything else.

SMELLS LIKE DEATH

Putrid smells don't always keep a hungry animal away. Some disgusting odors repel humans, while attracting other species.

Carrion flowers, also known as corpse or stinking flowers, release an odor that reeks of rotten flesh. Skunk cabbage has a foul odor, too. It smells like rotting meat. People may not want to get close, but to flies and beetles, it's heaven-scent!

skunk cabbage

Insects that dine on carcasses are attracted to these tricky stinkers. But the insects don't eat the plants. They pollinate them instead.

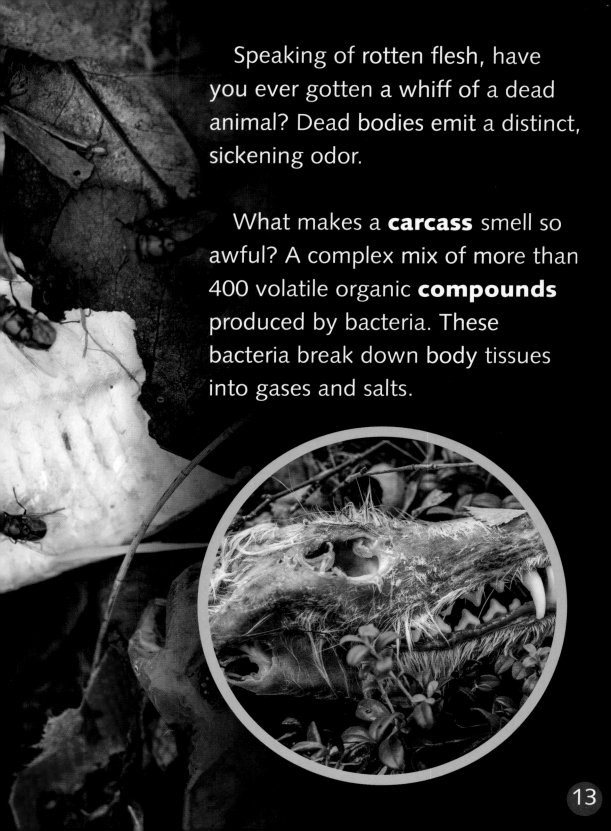

Speaking of rotten flesh, have you ever gotten a whiff of a dead animal? Dead bodies emit a distinct, sickening odor.

What makes a **carcass** smell so awful? A complex mix of more than 400 volatile organic **compounds** produced by bacteria. These bacteria break down body tissues into gases and salts.

Two of the more wel known compounds are cadaverine and putrescine. Both are **malodorous** molecule that may repel some animals and attract others.

Bears, raccoons, vultures, and other animals eat carrion. The smell of rotting meat doesn't make them tur up their noses or beaks

Lions, leopards, and other predators that usually hunt for fresh prey will eat carrion if they find it. It's an easy meal!

Humans, on the other hand, are naturally repulsed by the smell of cadaverine.

Eating rotten meat could cause illness or death. Being able to detect the smell of decay helped our hunter-gatherer ancestors avoid bad meat.

Meats, produce, and other foods that smell rotten should never be eaten. But the smell test doesn't work for everything. Many microbes that can cause illness do not produce detectable odors when they grow in food.

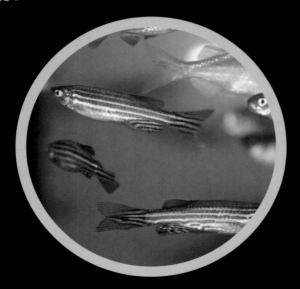

Scientists discovered that zebra fish have an olfactory receptor that makes the smell of cadaverine repulsive to them, much like humans.

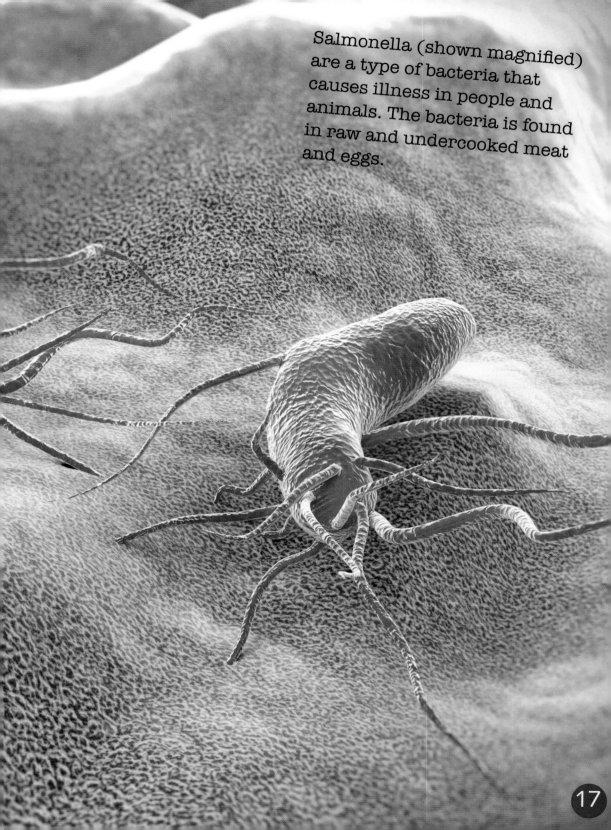

Salmonella (shown magnified) are a type of bacteria that causes illness in people and animals. The bacteria is found in raw and undercooked meat and eggs.

Cadaver dogs are trained to find and follow the scent of decomposing human flesh. These dogs help law enforcement officers locate crime victims.

Police officers and other professionals encounter dead bodies in their work. The odor of a human body **decaying** is so revolting, these workers may gag or vomit when they smell it. Even if they've smelled it many times before, there's just no getting used to that stench.

Researchers discovered five chemical compounds emitted by decomposing bodies that are unique to human flesh when compared to other animals. These compounds are part of a family of molecules called esters, which have the strong odors of pineapple, blackberries, and cherries. This research may help better train cadaver dogs to distinguish between human and animal remains.

Bacteria feed on food particles left behind after you eat.

PEOPLE STINK!

A live human can give off some seriously stinky smells, too. Bad breath, farts, and body odor can all assault your nose.

Why the stench? Blame the microbes again! Bacteria can build up in your mouth, around your teeth, and on your tongue if you don't brush regularly.

Bacteria feast on food in your gut. As they chow down, they release gas as waste. Most of the gas doesn't smell.

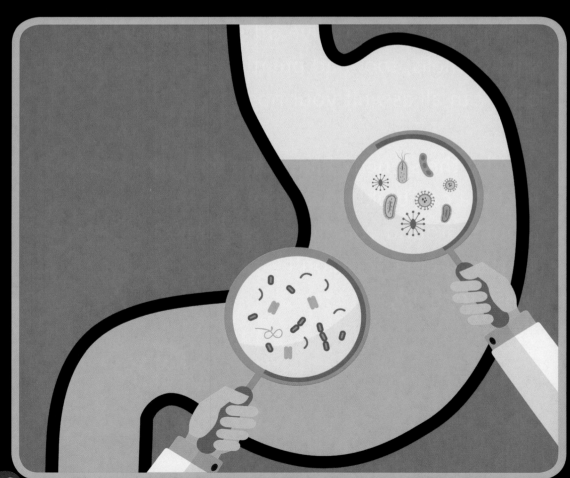

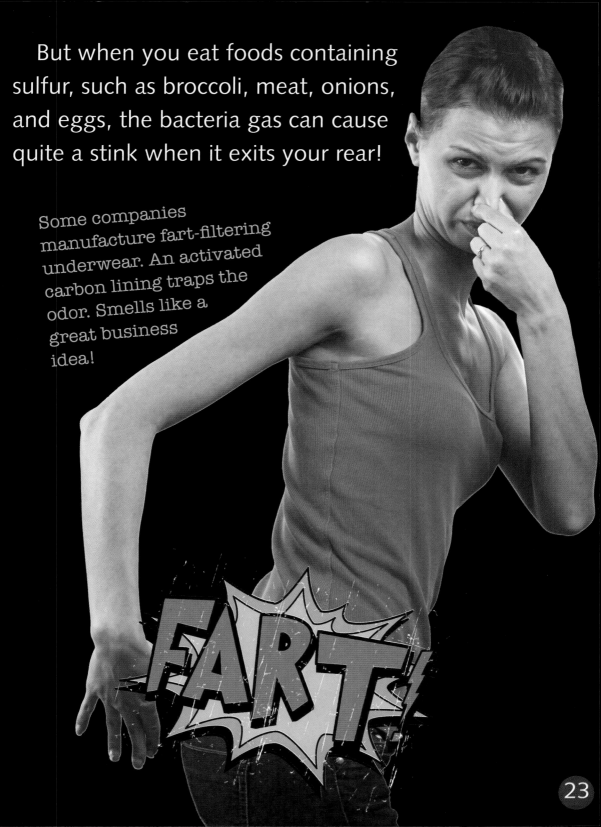

But when you eat foods containing sulfur, such as broccoli, meat, onions, and eggs, the bacteria gas can cause quite a stink when it exits your rear!

Some companies manufacture fart-filtering underwear. An activated carbon lining traps the odor. Smells like a great business idea!

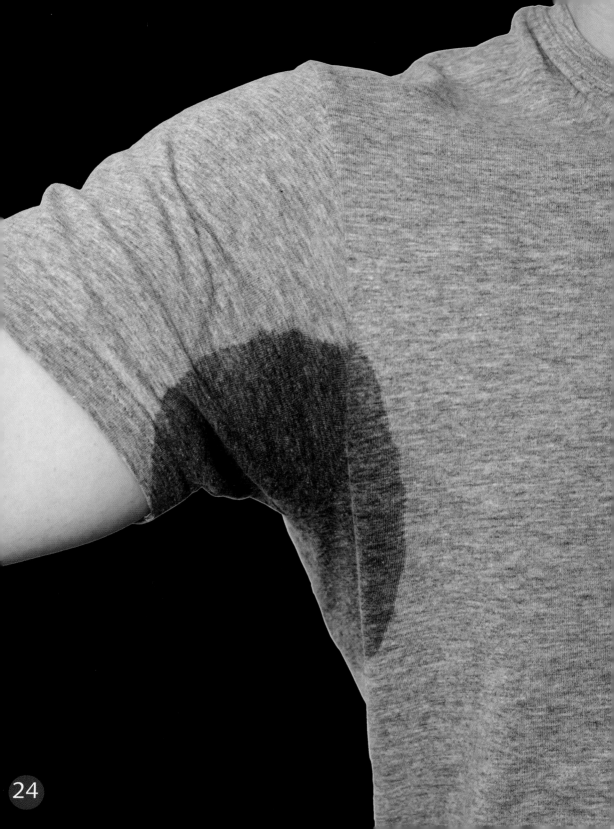

A **gaggle** of sweaty athletes in a crowded locker room can give off a stink that lasts long after they've left the building.

Human sweat is virtually odorless. So when you notice that you stink, it's not your fault. It's the bacteria living on your skin. These bacteria break down your sweat into acids. This is what causes the ripe odor.

Your body odor can be influenced by your gender, the foods you eat, your health, and medications you take.

Humans aren't the only stinkers. We can't forget about our smelly animal friends.

Skunks and lesser anteaters release a pungent spray when they feel threatened. The foul odor can be smelled for nearly a mile (1.6 kilometers) away.

Many other animals also have stinky defense systems. You won't want to get near them, much less eat them. And that's the point!

lesser anteater

If you or your pet is skunked, it could take some time to get rid of the funky skunky smell! No ordinary bath will do. The only way to really get rid of skunk scent is to allow the chemicals in the spray to be exposed to oxygen over time.

People may disagree about many things, but scientists say humans all over the world tend to universally agree on this: Spoiled food, dead bodies, and bodily wastes and fluids are disgusting.

And at the top of the world's gross list: poop. People everywhere say it's the grossest.

Poop is a combination of undigested food, bacteria, mucus, and dead cells. Bacteria produce sulfurous compounds that give your poop its icky odor.

Some scientists think nature made us find the smell of poop offensive so we won't eat it.

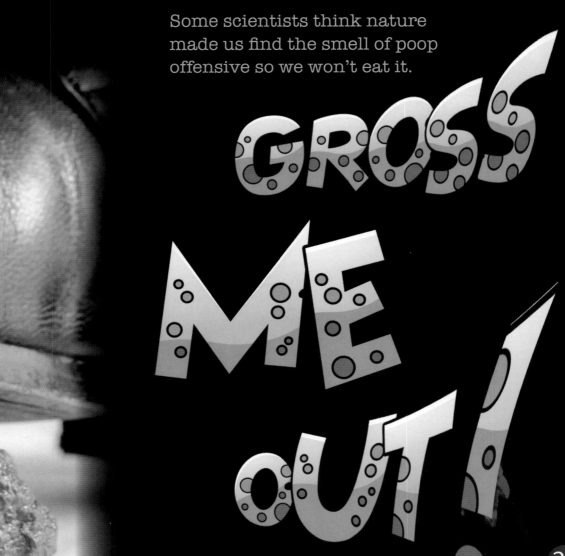

GROSS ME OUT!

GLOSSARY

carcass (KAR-kuhs): the body of a dead animal

compounds (KAHM-pounds): substances made from two or more chemical elements

decaying (di-KAY-ing): rotting or breaking down

gaggle (gag-uhl): a group or crowd

malodorous (mal-oh-durh-us): smelling very unpleasant

microbes (MYE-krohbs): microorganisms, especially bacterium causing disease or fermentation

pungent (PUHN-juhnt): having a strong or sharp smell or taste

putrid (pyoo-trid): decaying or rotting and emitting a fetid smell

INDEX

SHOW WHAT YOU KNOW

1. What is the only way to get rid of skunk stink?
2. Why might microbes make the food they grow on smell repulsive?
3. What are two compounds that make a decaying carcass produce a foul odor?
4. Why do some scientists think our poop smells bad to us?
5. What causes bad breath?

WEBSITES TO VISIT

www.chem4kids.com/files/elements/016_speak.html

http://easyscienceforkids.com/whats-that-smell-all-about-your-sense-of-smell

http://kidshealth.org/en/kids/experiment-smells.html

ABOUT THE AUTHOR

Darla Duhaime is a writer and purveyor of strange—and gross—facts from Sheffield, Vermont. When she's not writing, she enjoys picking wild berries, daydreaming, and cloud-watching. She likes to stay active and is known for keeping things interesting at family gatherings.

Meet The Author!
www.meetREMauthors.com

www.rourkeeducationalmedia.com

PHOTO CREDITS: Cover: rotten egg © chiraphan khongthim, vulture © Lebelmont, open mouth © Lightspring; pages 2-3 © riedjal; pages 4-5 dumpster © yingphoto, cartoon © Ron Leishman; page 6-7 © Patricia Chumillas; page 8-9 fly on egg © chiraphan khongthim, rotten pizza © mr.kie; page 10-skunk cabbage © steve52, page 11 © c. mokri - austria; page 12 © Tao Jiang, page 13 © Frozenmost; page 14-15 © Travel Stock; page 16-17 salmonella © Giovanni Cancemi, zebrafish © Kazakov Maksim; page 18-19 © Susan DeLoach; page 20 © Lightspring, page 21 © Giovanni Cancemi; pages 22-23 burp and fart logos © SFerdon, woman © offstocker, stomach with bacteria © graphicglobe; page 24 © Tamas Panczel - Eross, page 25 © Sign N Symbol Production: page 26 © Vladislav T. Jirousek, page 27 © Ultrashock; page 28 © Alfonso de Tomas, page 29 Gross Me Out Letters © Cory Thoman. All photos from Shutterstock.com

Edited by: Keli Sipperley

Cover and Interior design by: Nicola Stratford   www.nicolastratford.com

Library of Congress PCN Data

Gross Smells / Darla Duhaime
(Gross Me Out!)
 ISBN 978-1-68191-770-2 (hard cover)
 ISBN 978-1-68191-871-6 (soft cover)
 ISBN 978-1-68191-959-1 (e-Book)
Library of Congress Control Number: 2016932730

Rourke Educational Media
Printed in the United States of America, North Mankato, Minnesota

Also Available as: